World Series Champions: Houston Astros

Pitcher Roy Oswalt

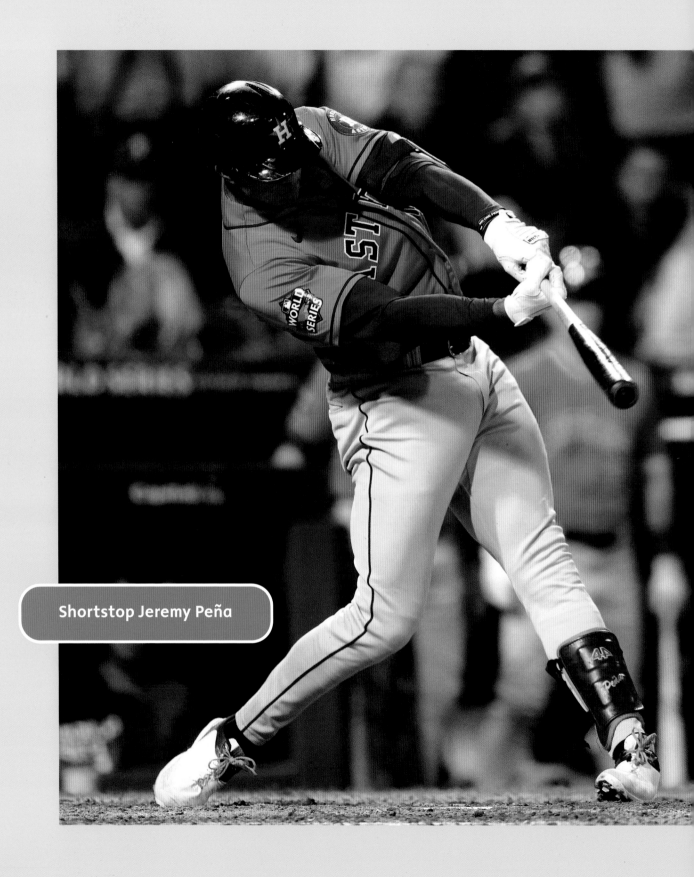

Shortstop Jeremy Peña

WORLD SERIES CHAMPIONS

HOUSTON ASTROS

JOE TISCHLER

CREATIVE SPORTS

CREATIVE EDUCATION / CREATIVE PAPERBACKS

Published by Creative Education and Creative Paperbacks
P.O. Box 227, Mankato, Minnesota 56002
Creative Education and Creative Paperbacks are imprints of
The Creative Company
www.thecreativecompany.us

Art Direction by Tom Morgan
Book production by Ciara Beitlich
Edited by Jill Kalz

Photographs by Alamy (Cal Sport Media), AP Images (Joe
Robbins/Icon Sportswire), Getty (Rob Carr, Stephen Dunn, Elsa,
Focus On Sport, John Grieshop, Rich Pilling, Louis Requena,
Daniel Shirey, Jamie Squire), Shutterstock (Sean Pavone)

Library of Congress Cataloging-in-Publication Data
Names: Tischler, Joe, author.
Title: Houston Astros / Joe Tischler.
Description: Mankato, MN : Creative Education and Creative
   Paperbacks, [2024] | Series: Creative sports. World Series
   champions | Includes index. | Audience: Ages 7-10 | Audience:
   Grades 2-3 | Summary: "Elementary-level text and engaging
   sports photos highlight the Houston Astros' MLB World Series
   wins and losses, plus sensational players associated with the
   professional baseball team such as Jose Altuve."-- Provided
   by publisher.
Identifiers: LCCN 2023008242 (print) | LCCN 2023008243 (ebook)
   | ISBN 9781640268234 (library binding) | ISBN 9781682773734
   (paperback) | ISBN 9781640009936 (pdf)
Subjects: LCSH: Houston Astros (Baseball team)--History--
   Juvenile literature. | World Series (Baseball)--History--Juvenile
   literature.
Classification: LCC GV875.H64 T57 2024 (print) | LCC GV875.H64
   (ebook) | DDC 796.357/64097641411--dc23/eng/20230306
LC record available at https://lccn.loc.gov/2023008242
LC ebook record available at https://lccn.loc.gov/2023008243

Printed in China

Pitcher Justin Verlander

CONTENTS

Home of the Astros

The city of Houston, Texas, is well known for its space program. It's home to the Johnson Space Center. The National Aeronautics and Space Administration (NASA) trains astronauts there. Houston is also home to the Astros baseball team. Fans watch them soar to new heights at a **stadium** called Minute Maid Park.

The Houston Astros are a Major League Baseball (MLB) team. They play in the American League (AL) West Division. Their **rivals** are the Texas Rangers. All MLB teams try to win the World Series to become champions.

Outfielder Jimmy Wynn

Naming the Astros

he Houston team started playing in the National League (NL) in 1962. They were first called the Colt .45s. In 1965, the team moved into a new domed stadium. The team owner wanted a new name to go with the city's space theme. Astros was picked. The new stadium became the Astrodome.

Pitcher Nolan Ryan

Astros History

The Astros waited nearly 20 years to make their first **playoff** appearance. They reached the NL Championship Series three times in the 1980s. But they lost them all. Pitchers Nolan Ryan and Mike Scott struck out a lot of batters.

Infielders Jeff Bagwell and Craig Biggio led Houston to three straight division **titles** in the 1990s. Together they were known as the "Killer B's." Each slugged many hits. Both are in the **Hall of Fame**.

The Astros reached their first World Series in 2005. They lost all four games to the Chicago White Sox.

Second baseman Craig Biggio

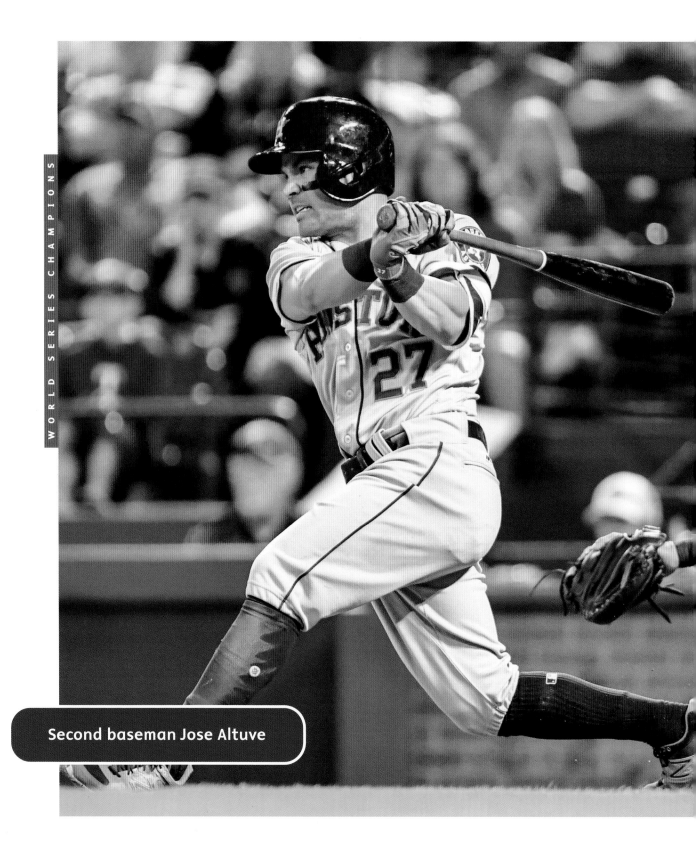

Second baseman Jose Altuve

Many losing seasons followed. Houston moved to the AL in 2013. Second baseman Jose Altuve sparked a winning trend. He led the AL in batting average three times. The Astros returned to the World Series in 2017. They faced the Los Angeles Dodgers. Houston won the series in seven games. It was their first championship! The Astros won the title again in 2022. They beat the Philadelphia Phillies in six games.

Other Astros Stars

The Astros have had many star pitchers. Roger Clemens, Dallas Keuchel, and Justin Verlander all won Cy Young Awards. The league's best pitchers win them.

José Cruz manned the outfield for many seasons. He was a two-time All-Star and won two **Silver Sluggers**. Third baseman Alex Bregman was a standout on both World Series championship teams.

Pitcher Roger Clemens

Outfielder Yordan Alvarez

**Y**oung stars Yordan Alvarez and Jeremy Peña were key to the team's 2022 title. Alvarez hit almost 100 home runs through four seasons. Peña was Most Valuable Player (MVP) of both the AL Championship Series and World Series. Fans hope to bring more championships to Minute Maid Park soon.

About the Astros

Started playing: 1962

. . . .

League/division: American
     League, West Division

. . . .

Team colors: dark blue and orange

. . . .

Home stadium: Minute Maid Park

. . . .

WORLD SERIES CHAMPIONSHIPS:

   2017, 4 games to 3 over
   Los Angeles Dodgers

. . . .

   2022, 4 games to 2 over
   Philadelphia Phillies

. . . .

Houston Astros website:
   www.mlb.com/astros

. . . .

Glossary

Hall of Fame—a museum in which the best players of all time are honored

· ·

playoffs—games that the best teams play after a regular season to see who the champion will be

· ·

rival—a team that plays extra hard against another team

· ·

Silver Slugger—an award given to the league's best hitter at each position

· ·

stadium—a building with tiers of seats for spectators

· ·

title—another word for championship

· ·

Third baseman Alex Bregman

Index